POWER THROUGH!

LET'S GO!

Stand STRONG
Part One: Coleman Learns to CENTER

Cool stuff for college (and life)!

A College Survival Guidebook With Practices For Your Success

Luckett Davidson

STAND UP FOR YOURSELF!

YOU GOT THIS!

Copyright © 2020 Luckett Davidson

A TouchStone Publication

ALL RIGHTS RESERVED

No part of this book may be translated, used, or reproduced in any form or by any means, in whole or in part, electronic or mechanical, including photocopying, recording, taping, or by any information storage or retrieval system without express written permission from the author or the publisher, except for the use in brief quotations within critical articles and reviews.

www.touchstoneguides.com, luckett@touchstoneguides.com

Limits of Liability and Disclaimer of Warranty:
The authors and/or publisher shall not be liable for misuse of this material.
The contents are strictly for informational and educational purposes only.

Printed and bound in the United States of America
ISBN: 978-1-7333434-0-4
Library of Congress Control Number: 2019919155

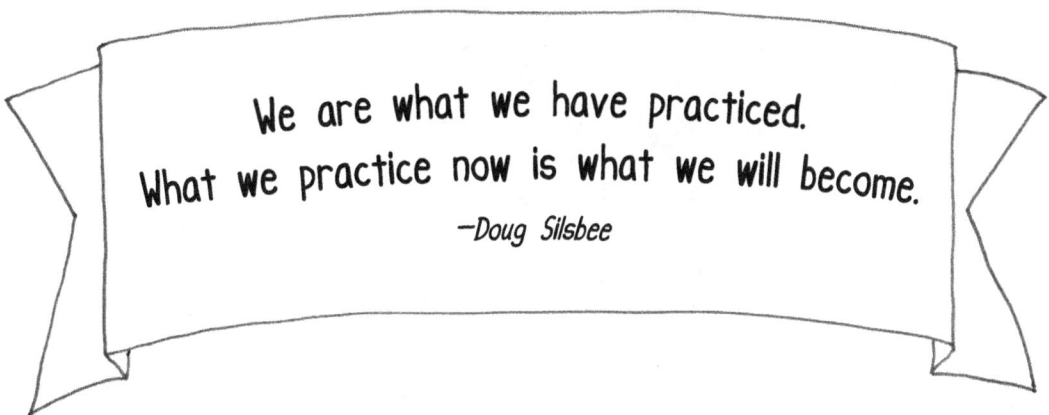

We are what we have practiced.
What we practice now is what we will become.
—Doug Silsbee

Stand STRONG, Part One

Coleman's Story and *Centering*

CONTENTS

Pages 2-13 The STORY

About **Coleman** and his first year in college

Pages 14-25 EXPLORE Your Own Story

Questions for you to think about and answer that'll help you do well in college and beyond

Pages 11 and 21 CENTERING

Learn to **CENTER** – You can practice at any time to feel more confident, calm and STRONG

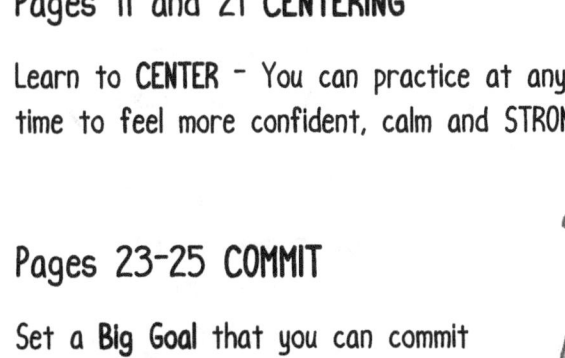

Pages 23-25 COMMIT

Set a **Big Goal** that you can commit to and plan some steps you can take to reach that goal

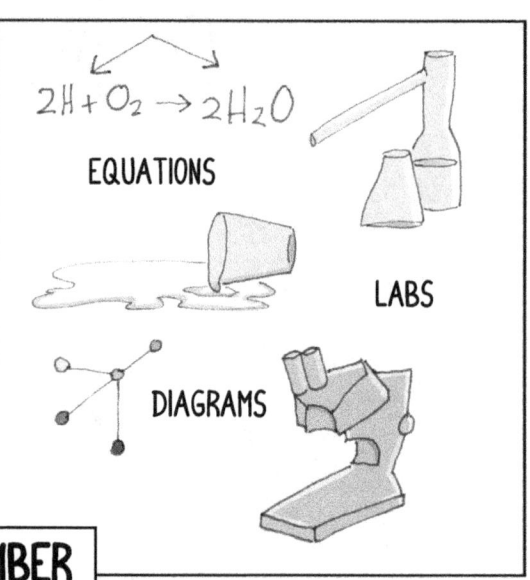

SEPTEMBER

OCTOBER

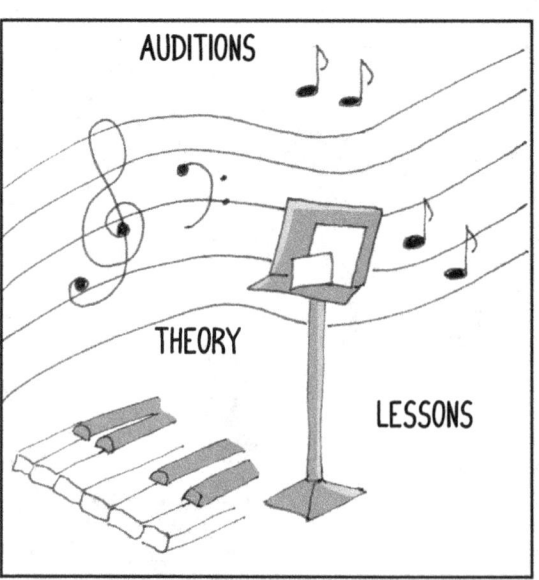

NOW
Stand up in your usual slouch.
Exaggerate a little.
THEN
Plant your feet hip-width apart.
Balance your weight front to back
and side to side.
Bring your chin parallel to the floor.
Straighten your spine from its base
to the top of your head.
Stretch into your full height and width.
Center your ears between your shoulders.
Look straight ahead, toward the horizon.
Breathe......Relax without moving......
Breathe.
Say
I CAN DO IT!

What habits and thoughts did you see in Coleman's story?
What else do you think he learned?
Write and draw and share.

EXPLORE YOUR OWN STORY
and
LEARN HOW TO CENTER

_____

(YOUR NAME)

Learns Centering

_____

(DATE)

Stand STRONG, Part One

As you answer the questions in the next few pages, look at your own habits of thought and action.

Consider: How do your thoughts and actions support your goal?

WHAT YOU'LL NEED:

* This book
* Willingness to think about your own story
* Pen or pencil
* Colored pencils or markers

WHAT YOU'LL DO:

* Make notes and images about what you are proud of and what you did to make it happen
* Reflect on what hasn't gone well and what you learned or could have
* Try Stand STRONG—a practice you can use at any time to feel more settled and confident
* Set a couple of Big Goals
* Plan some small steps you'll take right away to move toward your goals
* Share your thoughts and plans with someone who will support you

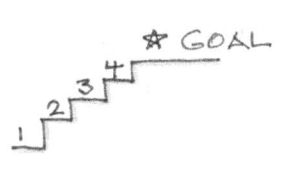   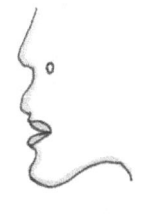

Name and draw one thing that went well for you recently.

Here are some things I thought of when we had this question in leadership group:

* I aced my math test
* I did better on my second chemistry test
* I got a scholarship in band

How did doing well feel? Write and draw.

These may help start your thinking:

- Proud
- Confident
- Deserving
- Lucky
- Competent
- Happy
- Brave
- Lighter
- Tingly
- Warm
- Energized
- More open in my chest

What did **YOU** do to make it go well?
Write and draw two or three actions **YOU** took.

Some things that worked for me:

* Asked for help
* Accepted help that was offered
* Kept saying "I can do it!"
* Managed my time
* Made lists and checked things off
* Learned to think of setbacks as temporary
* Celebrated small successes and progress
* Broke big goals down into smaller steps

Name and draw one thing that DIDN'T go well recently.

Some tough stuff I've experienced myself:

* I got a bad grade in a class
* I missed a major deadline
* I had a fight with my mom
* I messed up bad in a concert
* I lost a bunch of band music

What good stuff did you, or could you, learn from the thing that didn't go well? Write and draw.

One or more of these may fit for you:

* It's my attitude that counts
* Messing up is temporary
* Obsessing over mistakes doesn't make them better
* I do better when I go to class
* Sometimes there's more to learn by losing than by winning
* I remember other times when I got through something tough

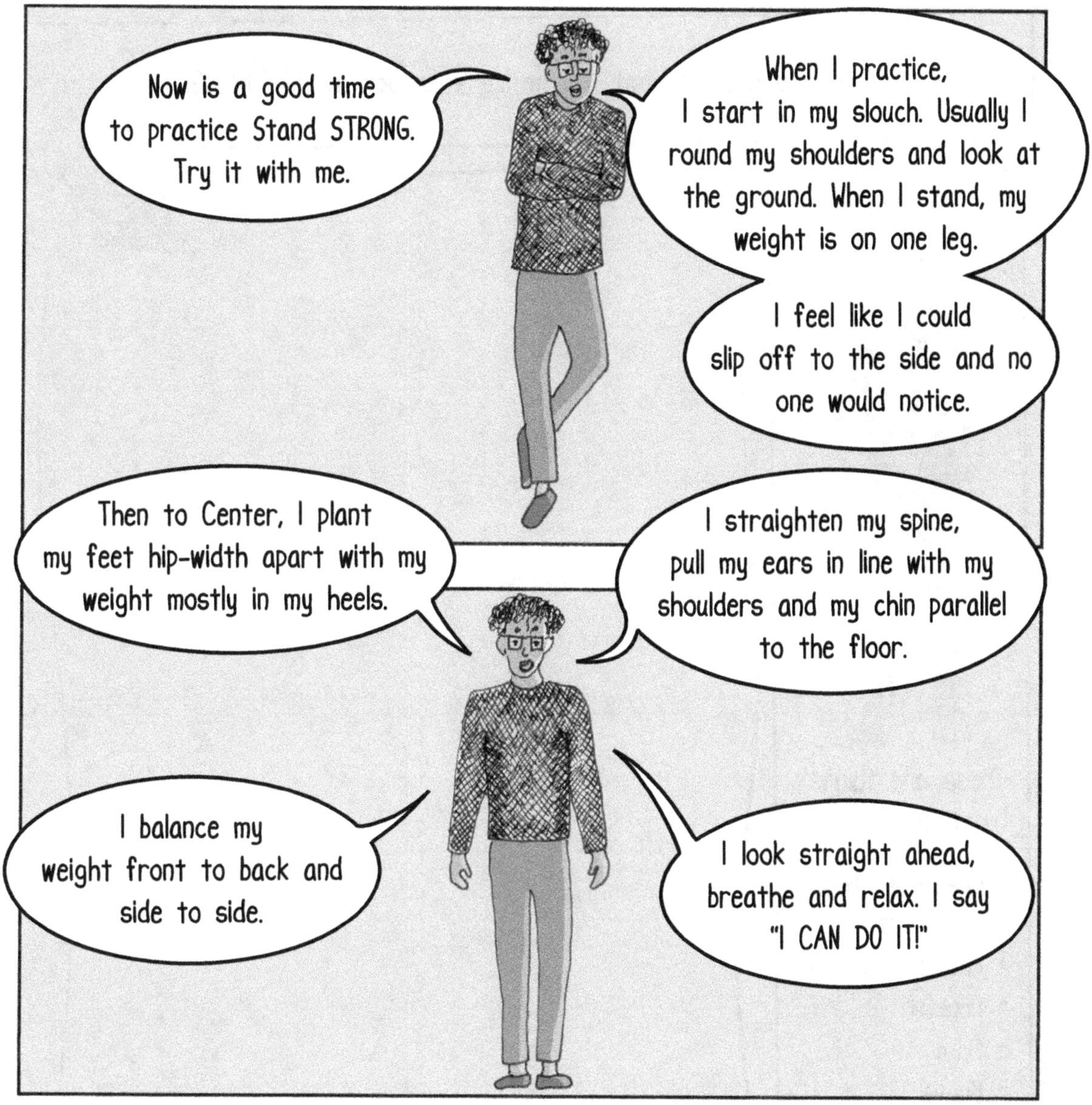

Write and draw what you notice when you Stand STRONG.

These are things I notice:

* Open eyes, heart and chest
* Easier breathing
* Hopeful
* Calm
* Brave
* Focused
* Energized

What's coming up where you need to Stand STRONG in the next month or so? Be specific.

Write and draw one or more **Big Goals** for the next few months.

These are my next Big Goals:

* Turn in all my papers and projects on time
* Get an A in chemistry
* Start a band
* Make three new friends

Pick ONE of your Big Goals and write it here:

Small doable steps make it possible to have early wins in progress toward your GOALS.

Write down all the things to do to make it happen. Start with what you can do right away on your own.

Break your ONE Big Goal down into smaller steps.

Which of your small steps will you commit to do right away? Write and draw and share:

Write a date to get it done and other details that will help you complete the small step you chose.

How can you reward yourself for completing this small step?

Who can you ask to help you reach your Big Goal?

YOU ROCK!

You've just completed Part One of Stand STRONG, a series that will help you navigate new experiences and stay calm under pressure and in the middle of major changes.

Practice Stand STRONG. Ask for help.
Break down big goals into smaller steps.
You can thrive in college and create the
life you want in college and beyond.

Draw a picture of yourself

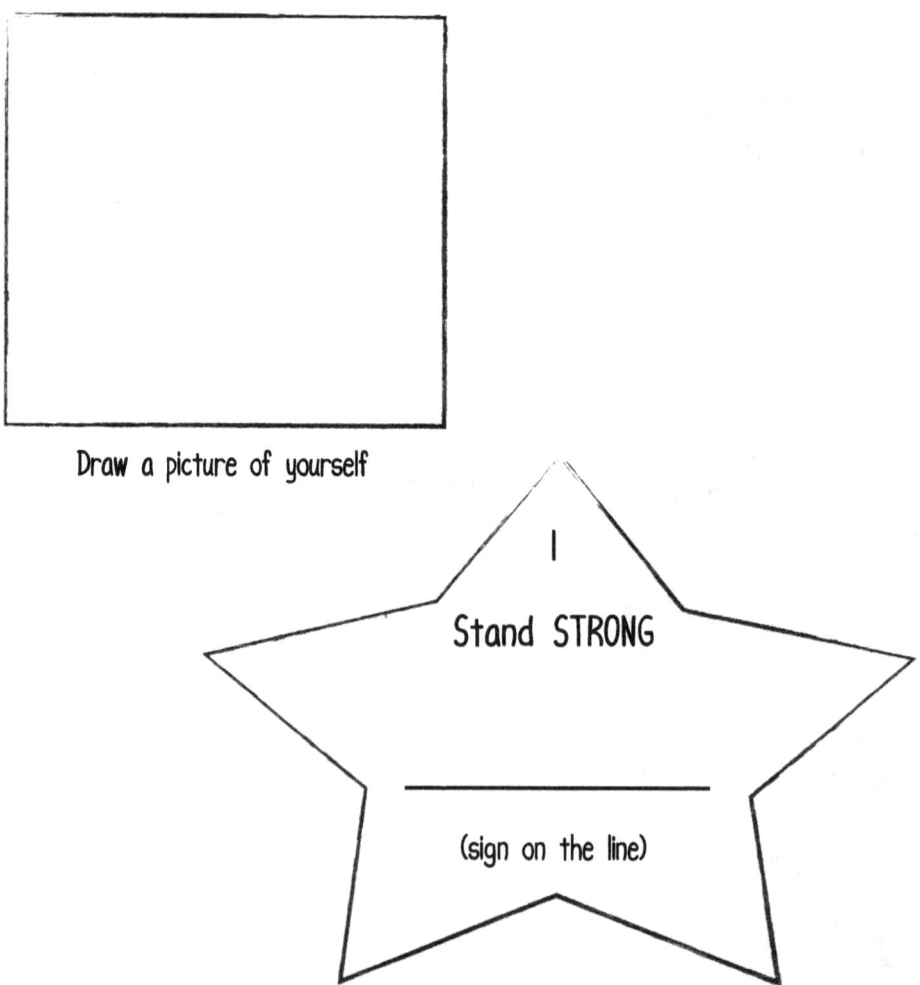

I
Stand STRONG

_____

(sign on the line)

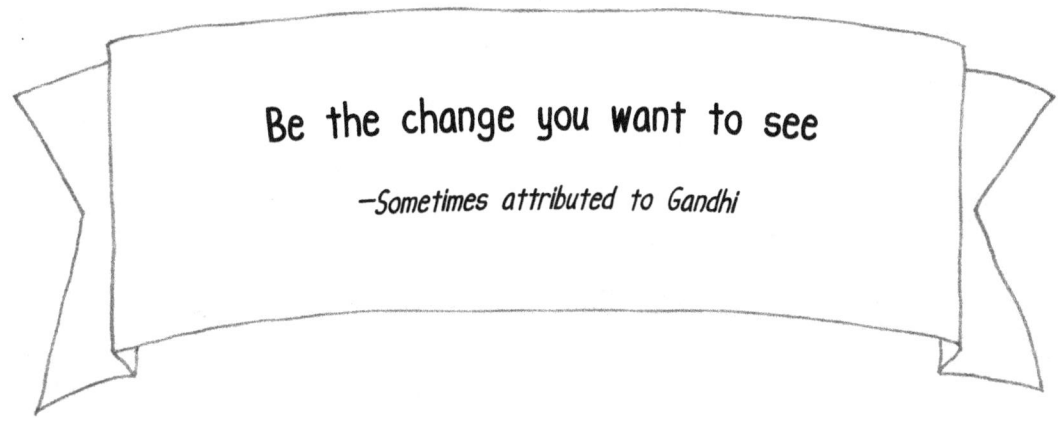

Be the change you want to see

—Sometimes attributed to Gandhi

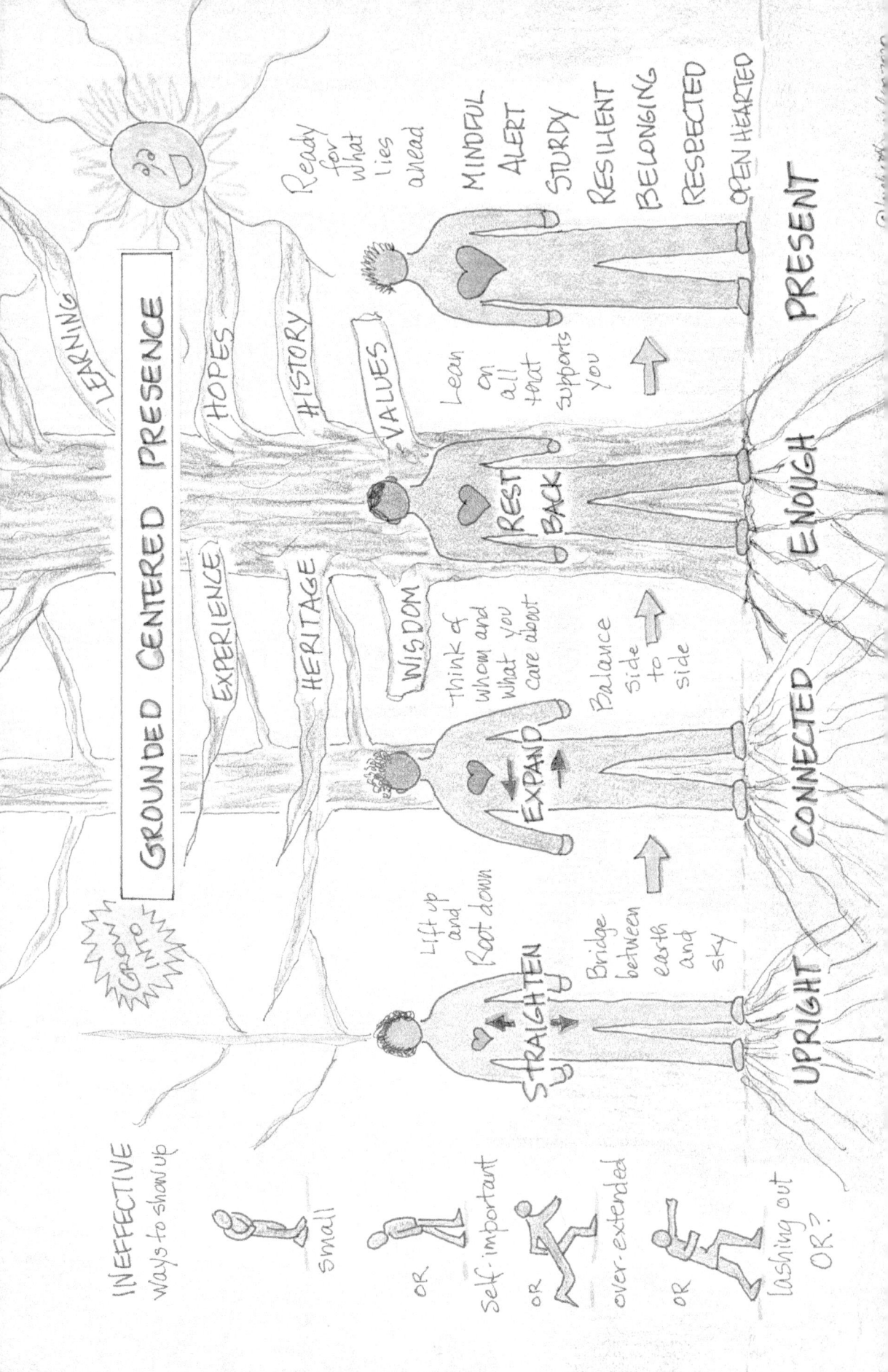

GRATITUDE

Kentucky Foundation for Women
Network Center for Community Change
Doug Silsbee & Bebe Hansen, Presence-Based Coaching®
Jill Adams and Change Makers, Jefferson Community and Technical College
Christy Metzger, First Year Experience, University of Louisville
Alexandra Thrustone, St. Francis School
Janelle Rae, Spalding University
Amy Hirschy, University of Louisville
Lisa Millsaps, Western High School
Tofte Lake Center and Liz Engleman
Jean Johnson and Barbara Hulburt
Lyedie Geer, Practicing Artists Lab
Grace Christiansen and David Temin
Guy Davidson and John Catlett
Elizabeth Neyman and Alex Haynes
Frank Steele, Editor
Karen Abney
Amari and Althea Dryden
Bethany Kelly, Publishing Partner
Stefan Merour, Graphic designer

Danica Novgorodoff, graphic novelist
Keith Look
Mikki and David Little
Amanda Blake, Embright
Shelton McElroy
Cassandra Webb
Mimi Zinniel
Liza Little
Jan Calvert
Ebony O'Rea
Nola and McGee Catlett
Jennie Jean Davidson
Steve Woodring
Witters
Rowing Sisters
Sarah Halley
Carey Goldstein
Jessica Bellamy
Pam Greenwell
Julie Wunderlin
Last Thursday Book Club

CITATIONS:

Centering, the practice:
Adapted from Doug Silsbee and Bebe Hansen, Presence-Based Coaching®

Safety, Connection and Respect
Adapted from Body=Brain®, Amanda Blake, Embright

Luckett Davidson, a leadership development coach, writer and illustrator, lives with her family in Louisville, Kentucky.

Luckett's take on the personal skills required for college survival is grounded in her studies and explorations in Presence-Based Coaching®, community organizing, the food industry, and fine arts as well as lived experience.

Touchstone Guides presents **Stand STRONG**, a series that supports students through the transition from high school to college. This unique, interactive series allows students to personalize their growth by reflecting and practicing new skills and habits of self-awareness and leadership presence.

In **Part One**, Coleman learns to Center and watches his confidence soar.

In **Part Two**, Will learns to ask Powerful Questions as he considers big and small decisions.

In **Part Three**, Shayla learns how the Accountability Pathway can help her make progress toward major goals.

Join them as they journey through the challenges of college and learn to build inner strength, seek support and stand strong!

Visit our website www.touchstoneguides.com to download the Stand Strong Tips for Session Leaders. These handy tips support those wishing to lead a small group! Posters are also available on the website for purchase.

Bulk and nonprofit rates are available. Contact us for more information at luckett@touchstoneguides.com.

Touchstone Guides explore the intersection of coaching skills, practices and accessible and memorable images. Compassion, resonance, grace and resilience are the touchstones of our work.

www.ingramcontent.com/pod-product-compliance
Lightning Source LLC
Chambersburg PA
CBHW081130080526
44587CB00021B/3816